Y0-ASY-881

EARTHQUAKES
By Ed and Ruth Radlauer

A Radlauer Geo Book

AN ELK GROVE BOOK
CHILDRENS PRESS®
CHICAGO

Created for Childrens Press
by Radlauer Productions, Incorporated

Cover: Mexico City, Mexico, 1985

Photo Credits: California Institute of Technology, Earthquake Engineering Research Laboratory, Department of Civil Engineering

The authors thank Donna Covarrubias, Assistant Librarian, Earthquake Engineering, California Institute of Technology, for help with illustrations.

Special thanks to John Hall, Ph.D., Department of Civil Engineering, California Institute of Technology, for authentication of the manuscript.

Library of Congress Cataloging-in-Publication Data

Radlauer, Ed.
  Earthquakes.

  (A Radlauer geo book)
  Includes index.
  Summary: Explores what causes earthquakes, where the tremendous power of a quake comes from, why they occur without warning, and whether it is possible to predict earthquakes.
  1. Earthquakes—Juvenile literature. 2. Seismology—Juvenile literature. [1. Earthquakes] I. Radlauer, Ruth, 1926-   . II. Title. III. Series.
  QE521.3.R28 1987   551.2'2   87-13772
  ISBN 0-516-07841-0

Copyright© 1987 by Regensteiner Publishing Enterprises, Inc.
All rights reserved. Published simultaneously in Canada.
Printed in the United States of America.

3 4 5 6 7 8 9 10 11 12 13 14 15 R 93 92 91 90

CONTENTS

	page
DISASTER	5
EARTH'S LAYERS	7
EARTHQUAKE LEGENDS	9
OCEANS SPREAD	11
TECTONICS AND EARTHQUAKES	13
AFTERSHOCKS	15
DANGERS IN THE AFTERMATH	17
HEROES	19
HAM HEROES	21
HISTORIC EARTHQUAKES	23
THE SEISMOGRAPH	25
MEASUREMENTS	27
RICHTER SCALE	29
LOCATING THE EARTHQUAKE	31
EARTHQUAKE DURATION	33
TSUNAMI	35
MAJOR EARTHQUAKE AREAS	37
WHEN WILL THE BIG ONE COME?	39
EARTHQUAKES AND YOU	41
GLOSSARY	42
INDEX	46
THE AUTHORS	48

What awesome force caused this disaster in Mexico City, Mexico?

4

DISASTER

It's 7:18 A.M. on September 19th, 1985. All the people in this huge city are going about their usual Thursday morning business or other activities. Suddenly, without any warning, within the space of just a few minutes, thousands of people die, and thousands are injured. Hundreds of the injured will die and many thousands of people have become homeless. Hundreds of buildings are destroyed. Some homes, many apartment buildings, and people's belongings lie in ruin. All this in just four minutes!

What awesome force has caused this terrible destruction? War? A bomb, perhaps? No, no war, no bomb. A hurricane, a flood, tornado, or a **tidal wave**? No, none of these.

Of course, we know what happened. Mexico City, Mexico, has been struck by an earthquake that measured a **magnitude** of 7.8 on the **Richter Scale**.

Why is it that sometimes, without warning, what some people call Mother Nature strikes with such violence? Where does the tremendous power in an earthquake come from? Can an earthquake be predicted? Where can people find shelter from an earthquake? Most importantly, what causes them?

tidal wave	unusually high wave caused by the action of ocean tides and wind—Tidal waves sometimes arrive onshore as the result of huge storms.
magnitude	numerical measure of strength
Richter Scale	series of numbers used to describe earthquake strength—See *magnitude* and page 29.

LITHOSPHERE

ASTHENOSPHERE

INNER SOLID CORE

OUTER LIQUID CORE

LOWER MANTLE

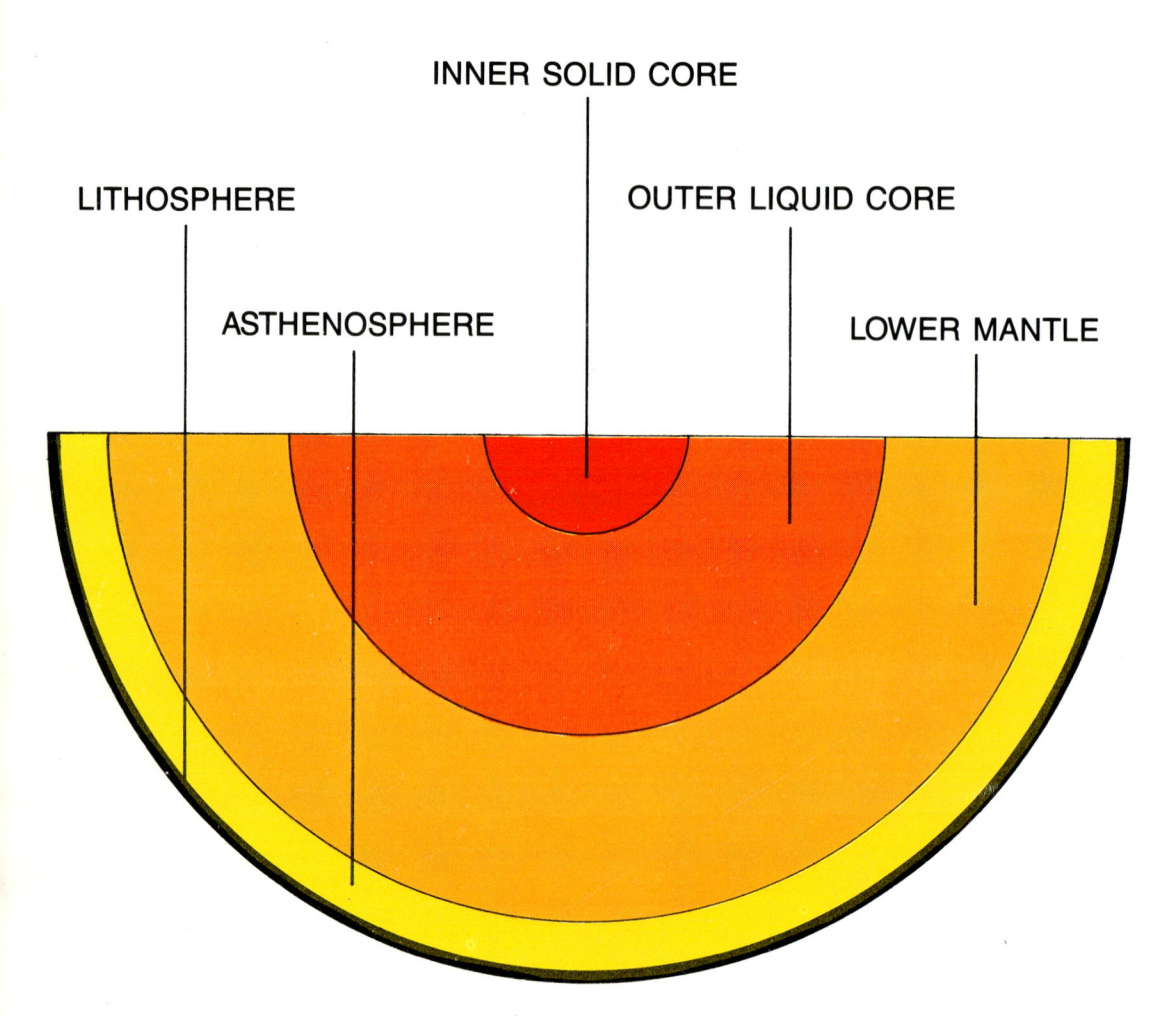

You can begin to understand earthquakes if you think of our planet as a huge ball made up of many layers.

EARTH'S LAYERS

If we could slice into the earth, we would see the layers that make up our planet. In the very center is a solid **core** almost 2,500 kilometers (over 1,500 miles) in **diameter**. This core is surrounded by other layers including a liquid core, a lower **mantle**, the *asthenosphere*, and finally, the *lithosphere* which includes the crust, the hard surface where we live. The lithosphere is about 30 kilometers (50 miles) thick and it floats on a fudgelike layer, the asthenosphere.

You can think of the lithosphere as a very thick shell with a number of cracks. Each area surrounded by crack lines is called a *plate*. These have been given names by scientists. Much of the United States sits on the North American Plate. Some of the earth's other plates are the Indian Plate and the Pacific Plate.

Unlike the cracked shell of an egg, the earth's plates move in relation to each other. *Plate tectonics* is a **theory** that explains many causes of earthquakes. But before the year 1912 and the work on plate tectonics by a German scientist, Alfred Wegener, people had strange ideas about earthquakes.

core	in this case, the central part of the earth below a depth of 2,900 kilometers—The core is thought to be molten iron with possibly a solid center.
diameter	length of a line drawn from edge to edge through the center of a circle or sphere
mantle	main bulk of the earth between crust and core
theory	group of ideas to explain a phenomenon

An ancient Japanese legend declared that a *namazu* (giant catfish) thrashed about underground and made the earth tremble unless a certain god kept it subdued with a stone mallet.

EARTHQUAKE LEGENDS

Many years ago some people believed a giant animal or god held the earth in its position among the sun, moon, and stars. If the animal or god moved or sneezed, an earthquake was the result. In one area, the **Celebes Islands**, people said the land was supported by a giant pig. Earthquakes occurred when the pig scratched its hide on a palm tree.

During a time thousands of years ago, the Greeks believed a giant man called Atlas supported the earth. The Greeks said earthquakes took place because Atlas shrugged his shoulders.

According to an early California Indian legend, seven sea turtles hold up the land, and when they get restless and want to move, the earth shakes and pulls apart.

Even the Old Testament of the Bible mentions earthquakes: "Then the earth shook and trembled; the foundations of hills moved and were shaken, because He was **wroth**."

Today we have scientific explanations for earthquakes, but even these theories change from time to time as scientists gain more understanding of earthquakes.

Celebes Islands group of islands near the country of Malaysia
wroth very angry

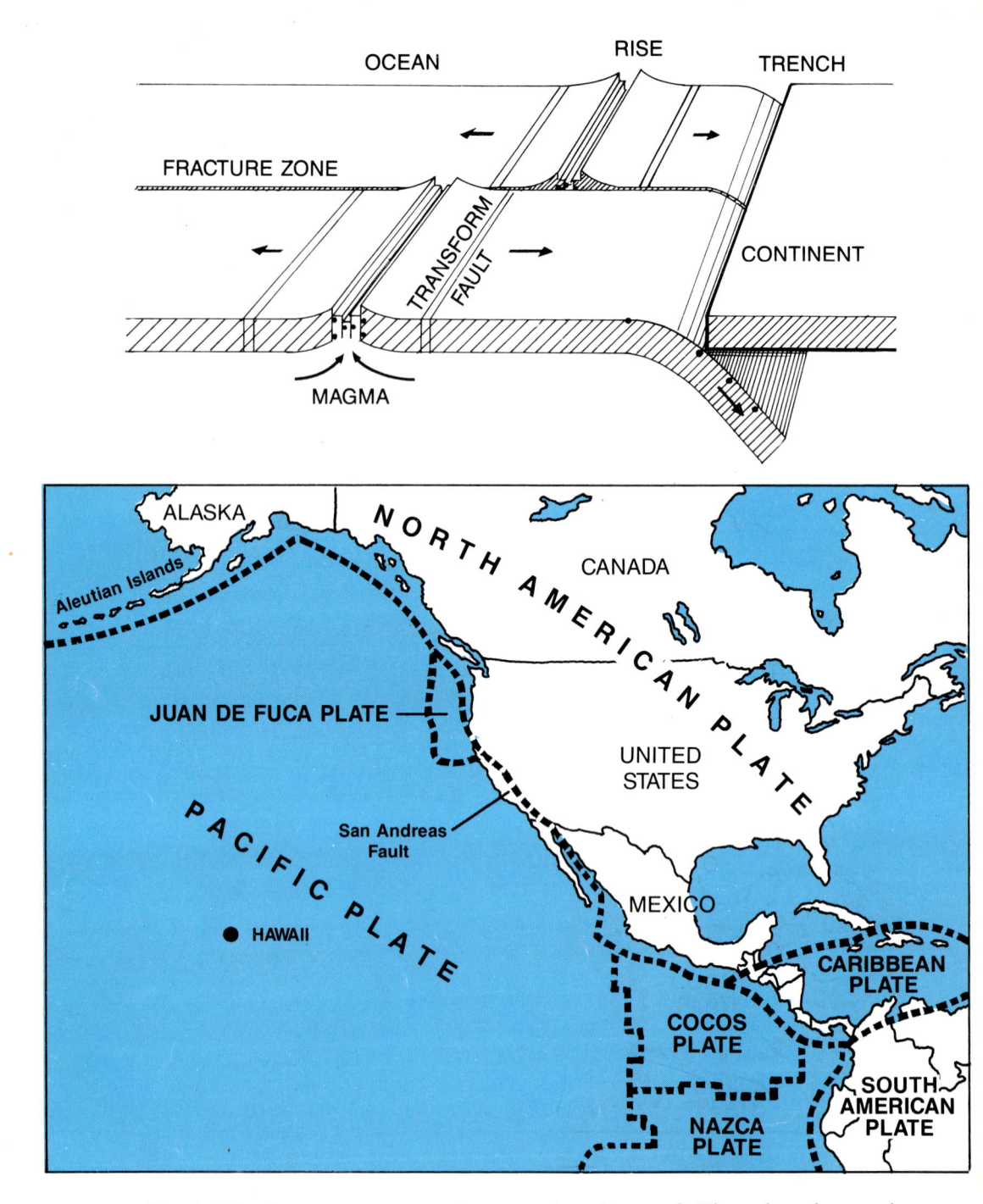

(Top) What's going on out there under the sea? The plate beneath the Pacific Ocean is spreading.

(Bottom) The Cocos Plate moved under the North American Plate and caused the 1985 earthquake in Mexico.

OCEANS SPREAD

Under some ocean areas, the plates are being driven apart at **spreading zones**, and from deep within the earth **magma** rises to fill in the gap. When this magma cools, new plate material is formed. In this way, the plates expand horizontally, or out from the sides, away from the spreading zone.

When the edge of a horizontally expanding plate meets another plate, something has to happen. At this meeting place, or **subduction zone**, one plate starts to go under another. This movement causes powerful forces to build up within the earth's lithosphere. From time to time, some of the forces caused by subduction are released in the form of an earthquake. The quake can be large or just a small **tremor**, depending upon the amount of force built up and released during this **interplate earthquake**.

The huge earthquake that took place in Mexico on September 19, 1985, is an example of one caused by subduction. Here, a part of the Pacific Plate called the Cocos Plate, meets the continental North American Plate. On September 19th, the pressure between the Cocos and the North American plates built up to a point where it was released as energy in a terrible earthquake.

spreading zone	area where plates are being driven apart and new plate material is formed from magma—See *magma*.
magma	molten rock beneath earth's surface that becomes lava when it erupts and rock when it cools
subduction zone	area where a plate dips under another one, usually an area where deep earthquakes occur
tremor	small movement within the earth's crust
interplate earthquake	one occurring at plate boundaries—Plate motion can be dipping or side-to-side. See *subduction zone*.

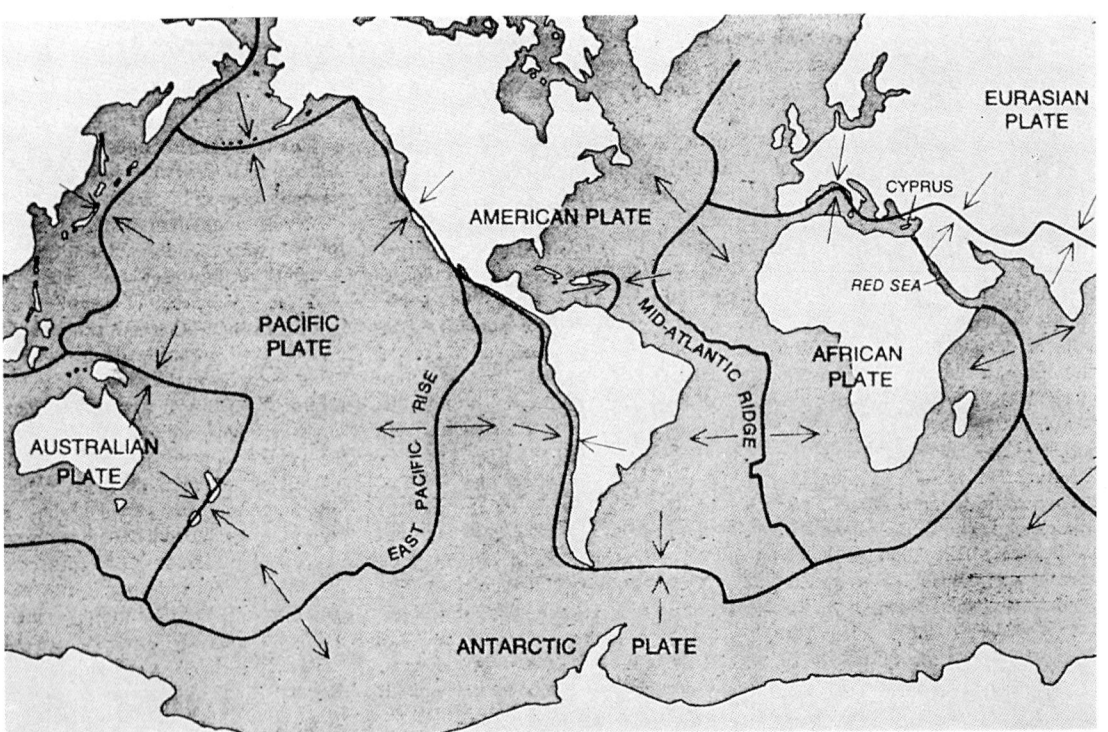

Before people understood earthquakes, they built cities without considering the dangers of living near **faults**. The Saint Francis Hotel in San Francisco, California, was built two years before the big quake of 1906. See page 22.

Arrows on the map show the directions of movement between major plates of the world.

12

TECTONICS AND EARTHQUAKES

Many earthquakes are caused by the forces that build up along a fault in the earth's surface. Faults, which can be thought of as enormous cracks in the earth, occur where two plates meet or where forces have caused a crack to develop within a plate. Any fault where movement has taken place in recent **geological time** is said to be an *active* fault. Many faults have had no movement for millions of years and are called *inactive*.

The movement of the earth's crust along an active fault builds up tremendous pressure in the earth's lithosphere. When such great pressure is released, there is an earthquake such as the one that occurred in San Francisco on April 18, 1906.

In an active fault, the forces that cause the earth to move build up continuously. Sometimes, if the fault cannot hold large pressures, the earth movement is also continuous, say a few centimeters per year. This is called **creep**.

However, if the crust involved in the active fault sticks together because of a great deal of **friction** and doesn't creep, huge pressures are built up. When these are great enough, rocks along the fault suddenly slip and release earthquake energy.

faults	series of fractures, parts of which have moved in relation to each other
geological time	span of the history of the earth as known today—about 4½ billion years
creep	slow earth movement that doesn't produce an earthquake
friction	sticking together of two surfaces because of their roughness

A building like this can collapse further if a strong **aftershock** occurs. San Fernando, California earthquake, February 9, 1971.

AFTERSHOCKS

Most big earthquakes are followed by aftershocks. These can be nearly as big as the main quake, or just mild **temblors**.

There are several theories about what causes aftershocks. Very likely, although pressure is released at most places on the fault during the earthquake, some locations may actually experience an increase in pressure. These locations may include extra strong points on the fault that did not slip or other areas where the initial pressure was too low to cause movement or slip. After some time, the increased pressure may be released by further fault motion. Such movements *after* the main quake are felt as aftershocks.

Aftershocks may be felt minutes, days, even weeks after a large earthquake. The Aleutian Islands in Alaska had an earthquake on February 24, 1965. During the 24 days following this quake, there were more than 750 aftershocks strong enough to be measured by distant **seismographs**. A seismograph *near* the area where the quake occurred probably would have measured *thousands* of aftershocks.

aftershock	lesser temblor following a big quake
temblor	shaking of the earth
seismograph	instrument that records the earth's motions during a seismic event in the form of a written record—See *seismic event*.

What happens *after* an earthquake can be worse than what happens *during* the quake. Downed electric lines can be fatal.

DANGERS IN THE AFTERMATH

A strong earthquake is a frightening experience. People are grateful when it seems to be over. But after a strong temblor, there are many other hazards.

Besides fallen electric lines there is the possibility of fire and explosion. If leaking gas is trapped underground, it can be **detonated** like a bomb if there is a spark or flame present.

There is more. If people have been killed, they must be found and buried. Injured people need to be located and given first-aid or taken to hospitals. Such efforts are important immediately after a quake.

Some dangers exist for a longer time. People may have to live without electricity, public water supplies, or well water for days or weeks. The very communication services needed to send for help may be destroyed, leaving people uncertain and anxious to let relatives know what has happened.

Other hazards in the aftermath may also cause illness or death. If both sewer lines and drinking water lines are **ruptured**, water **contamination** can occur. This is a long-term problem. People who drink contaminated water may develop **typhoid fever** or **cholera**, both life-threatening illnesses.

aftermath	time following a disastrous event
detonated	set off to explode like a bomb
ruptured	torn open
contamination	in this case, fouling of water so that it's no longer fit to drink
typhoid fever	illness causing diarrhea, headache, fever, and possible death
cholera	illness similar to typhoid fever, caused by water which is contaminated with human or animal wastes—See *typhoid fever* and *contamination*.

An earthquake brings out many kinds of heroes. Mexico City, Mexico, 1985.

HEROES

Quite often after a big earthquake, many uninjured people become heroes. They work day and night with machinery, tools, and bare hands to locate those caught under the rubble. These people listen for the slightest sound of human life: cries, tapping, moaning. Sometimes this work has to be carried on in a place where danger still exists, perhaps under a damaged bridge or hospital.

Some of these heroes are government employees such as police and fire fighters. Many are not, but all rescue workers risk their own safety for the sake of the injured. Medical people have been known to work almost continuously with little or no rest for days, caring for those who need help. Rescue workers must be ready for surprises, terrible or pleasant. After the Mexico City earthquake, workers dug out two dead girls but their puppy was unhurt.

Days after the quake, heroes managed to rescue eight newborn babies from the ruins of two hospitals. They were still alive!

Earthquakes cause countless injuries that require blood transfusions. People who donate blood to help such victims are surely **unsung** earthquake heroes.

An earthquake is always followed by cries for medical supplies, food, and water. But who hears the cries?

unsung   not recognized nor heard of

After an earthquake there may be radio cries for help. In California, **ham radio operator** Bob Soltys' hobby turned into an important public service when he became a radio link between people in Mexico City and their relatives in the U.S.

HAM HEROES

The quake is over. The electric power is off. Radio and television stations have become silent because of the loss of electricity, or even the loss of **transmitting towers**. Telephones are dead because poles and wires are on the ground. How can the people who survive the quake call for help?

It's time for the ham radio operator to contact the outside world. Ham operators can do this because many have batteries to power their radios. Some even have their own **power supplies**.

The ham's first job is to report to the world what has happened. Next he or she reports on damage, deaths, and injuries, if known. This is followed by a call for help. What kind of help? Medical supplies, additional doctors and nurses, clothing, food. Also needed are trained persons such as engineers who know how to take down damaged buildings without causing more injuries.

Following a big quake, many ham operators stay by their **rigs** for days, helping people far from the quake get information about friends and relatives. Only when regular communication is back in working order does the ham operator say "**73**" and **sign off** the rig.

ham radio operator	person with permit to operate a radio capable of sending messages a long distance
transmitting towers	tall structures from which radio and television messages are sent
power supplies	electricity-generating machines, usually powered by gas or diesel fuel
rig	in this case, a ham radio
73	ham radio way of saying "goodbye"
sign off	in this case, shut down the radio

Many earthquakes have made history. In 1906, the two-year-old Saint Francis Hotel in San Francisco, California, had to be destroyed because of earthquake damage.

HISTORIC EARTHQUAKES

Fortunately most earthquakes are small and soon forgotten. But many are not, and the story of these is in the history books.

Among the earliest recorded is an earthquake that shook Shensi, China, and killed about 830,000 people during the year of 1556. This could be the greatest number of earthquake casualties in recorded history. In 1882 the city of Aleppo, Italy, was destroyed and 22,000 people met their deaths. China was struck again in 1920 in Kansu **Province** and 200,000 people died. Yet another quake which took place around Tangshan, China, in 1976 is said to have killed 650,000 and injured 780,000 or more.

In the city of San Francisco at 5:12 A.M. on April 18, 1906, a section of rock on the **San Andreas** fault slipped. This break caused huge **seismic waves** to spread in all directions. The resulting earthquake and fire killed 453 people, injured many more, and destroyed about 28,000 buildings.

On March 27, 1964, the most powerful quake in North America, 8.3 on the Richter Scale, shook Anchorage, Alaska. Thirty blocks of the city were destroyed and about 130 people were killed.

Some say that today's world, with its huge cities, crowded neighborhoods, and tall buildings, may see earthquake disasters as bad as any on record.

province   area similar to a state such as those in the United States

San Andreas   fault along the west coast of Mexico and the U.S., located where the North American and Pacific Plates meet—See Glossary and *fault* and *plate*.

seismic wave   wave of energy traveling through the earth's interior or on its surface

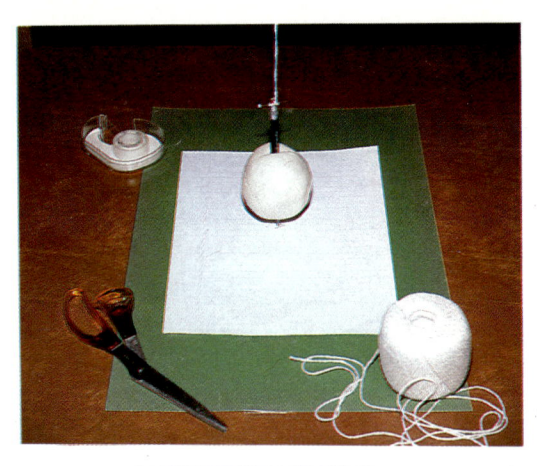

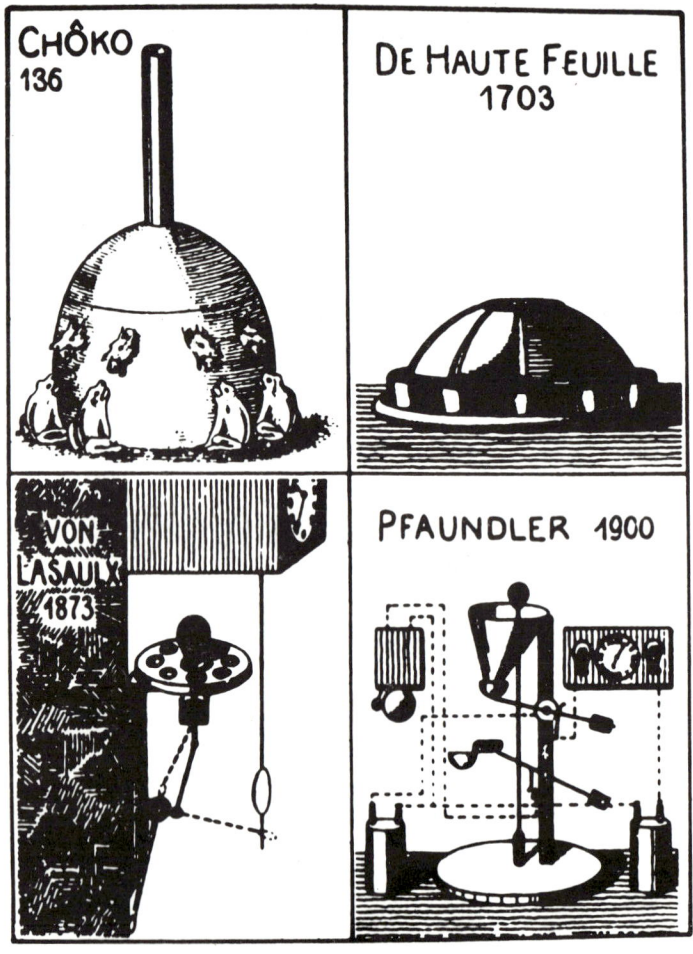

(Top) How does a seismograph work? Make one and find out.

(Bottom) Early motion-detection instruments.

24

THE SEISMOGRAPH

You can understand the workings of a seismograph by making one. Here's how. With your parent's permission, tape a piece of notebook paper to a table.

Tie a string about the length of your arm to the eraser end of a soft lead pencil. Weight the pencil by making a ball of clay. Push the pencil through the center of the clay until the point shows. Have a friend with a very steady hand hold the pencil and string above the paper on the table. The pencil lead should just barely touch the paper.

Now you provide the earthquake, in this case, a "tablequake." Tap the side of the table gently. As the table quakes and moves, the end of the pencil writes a **seismogram** of the event on the paper.

If you tap the table harder and harder, you notice that the pencil lines recording the **seismic event** travel farther from side to side because the magnitude of the tablequake you've created is greater.

The seis*mograph* instrument was your friend's steady hand, the string, and pencil. The lines, called *traces*, left by the pencil, are the seis*mogram*, the written record of the tablequake.

seismogram   written record of a seismic event—See *seismic event.*
seismic event   occurrence related to an earthquake

People have many ways to describe the strength of an earthquake and the damage it does.

(Top) San Fernando, California. (Bottom) Turnagain Arm, Alaska.

26

MEASUREMENTS

In describing an earthquake one can use words such as terrible, scary, very, very bad, or mild and hardly noticeable.

The *Mercalli Scale* describes earthquake intensity in Roman numerals from *I* to *XII*. For example, a Mercalli intensity of I means hardly anybody felt it. VII means everybody ran outdoors, even though that's dangerous, but damage was slight. Mercalli XII means there was total damage.

Another way to tell about an earthquake is with **statistics**. You can tell about the number of deaths as in the China quake of 1556 where over 800,000 people died. You could also add the number of injuries to further describe the seismic event.

Describing damage can be a way of reporting the effects of a quake. You could say 300 buildings were completely destroyed and hundreds more were badly damaged. You may want to report some information on how many people were left homeless. Adding up costs of the property destroyed gives more information.

Of course all the facts just listed are useful. But **seismologists** wanted ways to **quantify** the magnitude of seismic events.

statistics	numbers for things such as damage and injuries related to a seismic event
seismologist	person who studies seismic action
quantify	measure in a logical way, usually with numbers

The Richter Scale, developed in 1935 by Charles Richter (1900-1985), describes earthquake magnitudes in numbers. Mexico's 1985 quake measured 7.8 on this scale.

RICHTER SCALE

Earthquakes around the world vary from weak ones to some thousands of times more powerful. Because the strength varies so much, a special series of numbers is used to describe these events. The numbers most seismologists use are those of the Richter Scale. On this scale, a magnitude of 2.0 or 3.0 indicates a very weak earthquake, while an 8.0 means a very strong one.

In the Richter Scale, each number going up the scale means an earthquake of that magnitude releases 30 times as much energy as the one with a number just below it. For example, a Richter Scale 7.0 would release 30 times as much as a 6.0, but an 8.0 would release 900 times as much as a 6.0.

And, while it's not possible to feel an earthquake of magnitude 1.0, the quake that destroyed San Francisco in 1906, before the Richter Scale was developed, is believed to have measured 8.25.

There are several reasons for wanting to know the magnitude of an earthquake. Information from previous quakes can help people judge how much damage may have occurred during a very recent quake. Knowledge of the magnitude of previous quakes in a given area can help people decide on what areas may present a danger to new buildings and construction. Accurate earthquake information also helps people learn how to construct buildings that can better resist earthquake damage.

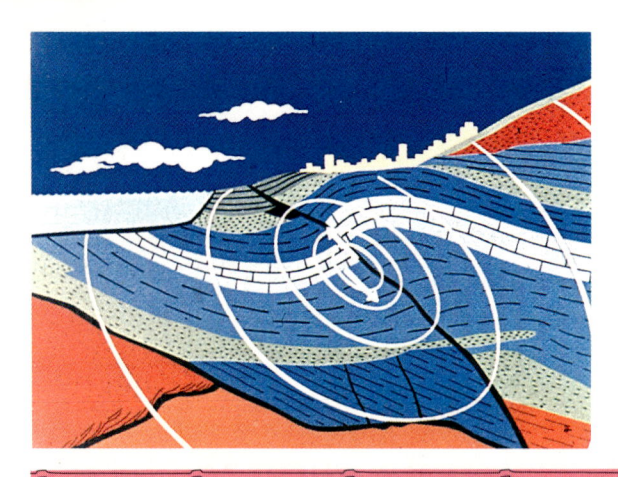

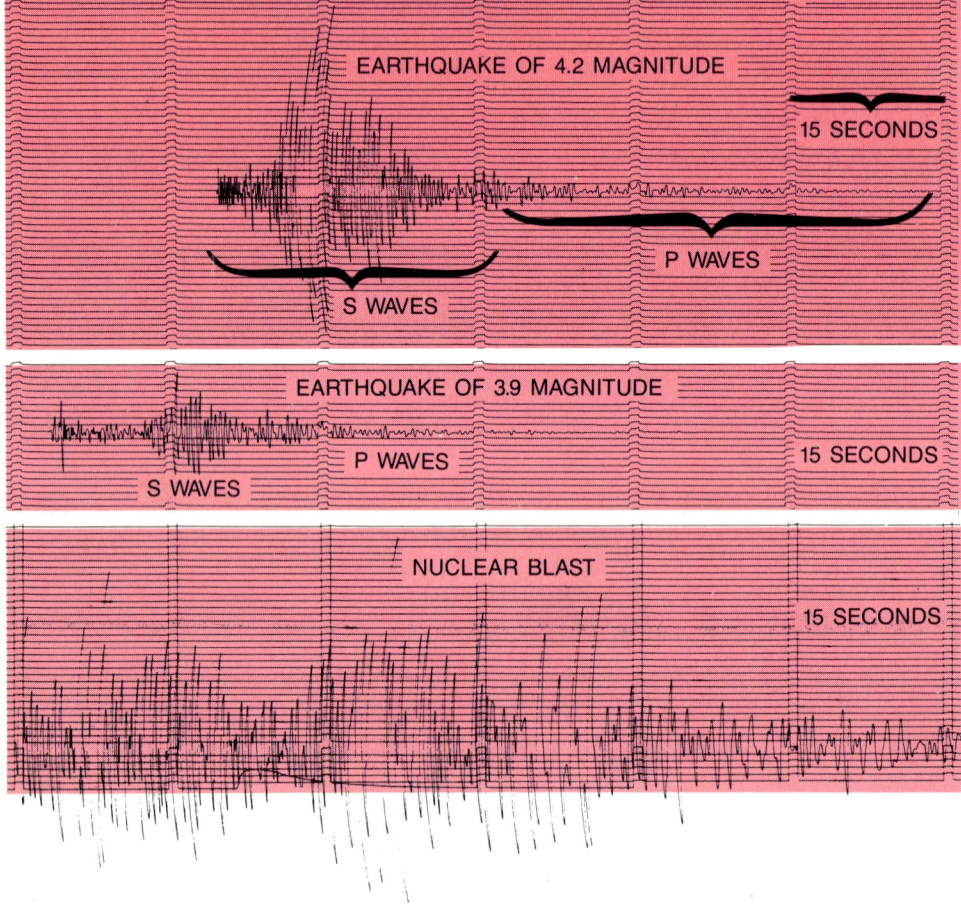

(Top) Heavy black line in the diagram shows a fault. White lines are waves moving out from the **epicenter** of an earthquake.

(Bottom) Seismologists learn much from the traces on seismograms.

30

LOCATING THE EARTHQUAKE

You may feel an earthquake of 3.2 magnitude or more, but you don't know *exactly* where the quake's epicenter and **focus** are located.

The focus of a quake can be anywhere between the earth's surface and a depth of 280 kilometers (450 miles). During the quake, several kinds of **body waves** move outward from the epicenter. The first and fastest moving is the **primary** or **P wave**. The P wave **p**ushes rocks and materials ahead of itself and can sometimes be heard as a low rumble. Next comes the slower moving **secondary** or **S wave**. The S wave **s**hoves rocks and materials from side to side. Still other waves are generated that travel on the surface of the earth.

Seismologists far from an earthquake's epicenter use information from a seismogram to measure the difference in arrival times of the first P and S waves at the seismograph station. With this information and knowledge of how fast the P and S waves travel in the earth, the distance to the epicenter can be found. Data from several different stations permit the epicenter's location to be pinpointed. Seismologists also use the strengths of the waves, as seen on the seismogram, to determine the quake's magnitude.

epicenter	point on the earth's surface just above quake's focus—See *focus*.
focus	starting point of the tear or rupture in earth's surface at the beginning of a quake
body wave	wave sent out by an earthquake which travels *through the earth* as opposed to surface waves that travel on the earth's surface
P wave, primary	first and fastest body wave after the quake—P waves contract and release material in line with their forward movement through the earth. See *S wave*.
S wave, secondary	body wave that follows P wave—S waves actually shove rocks and other material to the right and left of their direction of motion. See *P wave*.

This clock fell during the 1971 San Fernando earthquake. It gives us an idea of when the quake happened but not how long it lasted.

EARTHQUAKE DURATION

If you had been in an earthquake and somebody asked how long it lasted, you could say, "It seemed like forever." This may be a good description of earthquake **duration**. But it's not accurate, because your feelings might be very different from someone else's.

Duration is important in measuring earthquakes because the **bracketed duration** is as responsible for damage as the earthquake's strength of shaking.

To measure duration, seismologists decide on a level of shaking that marks the start of the bracketed duration when this level is exceeded and the end of it when the shaking dies down below this level. For these strong motions near the earthquake's epicenter, **accelerographs** are used because the sensitive seismographs would be overloaded. The level of shaking that is usually chosen to mark the start and end of the bracketed duration is above an **acceleration** of .05 **g**. Most damage occurs during this period.

So if you are in an earthquake, remember, the powerful vibrations of an earthquake will decrease in less than a minute, and quite often in less than fifteen seconds. Even so, a very powerful quake can do a lot of damage in less than 10 seconds.

duration	in this case, how long an earthquake lasts
bracketed duration	length of time that earthquake level of shaking is above .05g—See g.
accelerograph	instrument to measure the acceleration of an object—In this case, the object is a portion of the earth's surface. See *acceleration*.
acceleration	gaining of speed—Negative acceleration means loss of speed, commonly called *deceleration*.
g	acceleration of a falling body—See more in Glossary.

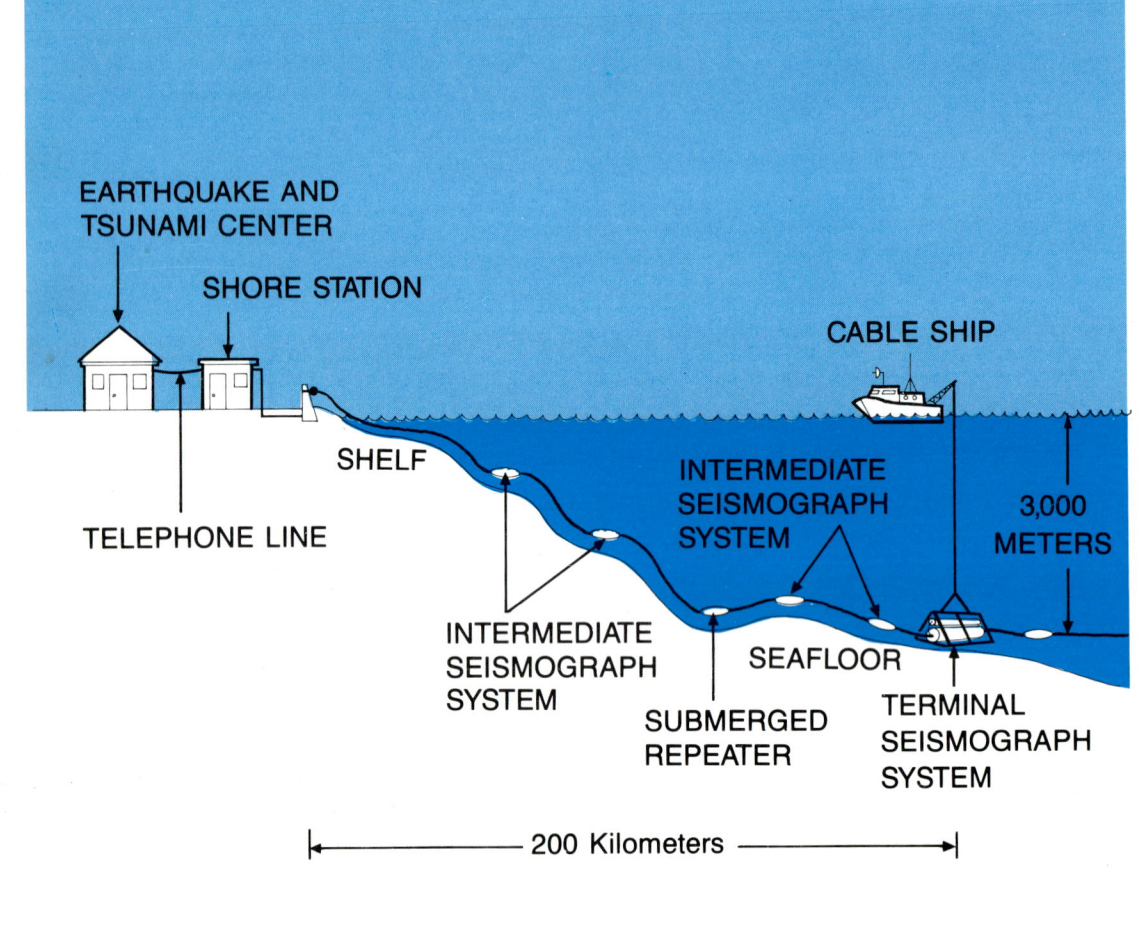

EARTHQUAKE AND TSUNAMI CENTER
SHORE STATION
CABLE SHIP
SHELF
INTERMEDIATE SEISMOGRAPH SYSTEM
3,000 METERS
TELEPHONE LINE
INTERMEDIATE SEISMOGRAPH SYSTEM
SEAFLOOR
SUBMERGED REPEATER
TERMINAL SEISMOGRAPH SYSTEM
200 Kilometers

On June 15, 1896 a so-called tidal wave some 24 meters high swept ashore on the island of Honshu, Japan. About 26,000 people drowned. Tsunami warning centers have been developed to save lives.

TSUNAMI

On March 28, 1964, what seemed to be another tidal wave swept over Crescent City, California. There was $104 million in damage and 119 people died.

Now we know these weren't tidal waves, and they had nothing to do with tides. These were giant sea waves called *tsunamis*, caused by an underwater seismic event.

Throughout history, tsunamis have struck without warning. And since they may be generated by a quake hundreds or thousands of kilometers from where they strike, there is no way to tell when one will arrive onshore.

A tsunami moving across the sea may look like a wave no more than one meter high, so people on a ship could not detect the movement. But once the tsunami gets to where water is shallow, near land or at the mouth of a bay, the wave rises quickly and suddenly floods the area.

Of course not all underwater quakes produce these "killer waves," as some people call them. But the type of earthquakes that produce vertical motion at the bottom of the sea are very likely to cause a tsunami.

Warning centers in Hawaii, Hong Kong, China, and other places observe underwater seismic events. These observations help predict where and when tsunamis might occur. Given time and warning, people can protect themselves from these sudden invasions from the sea.

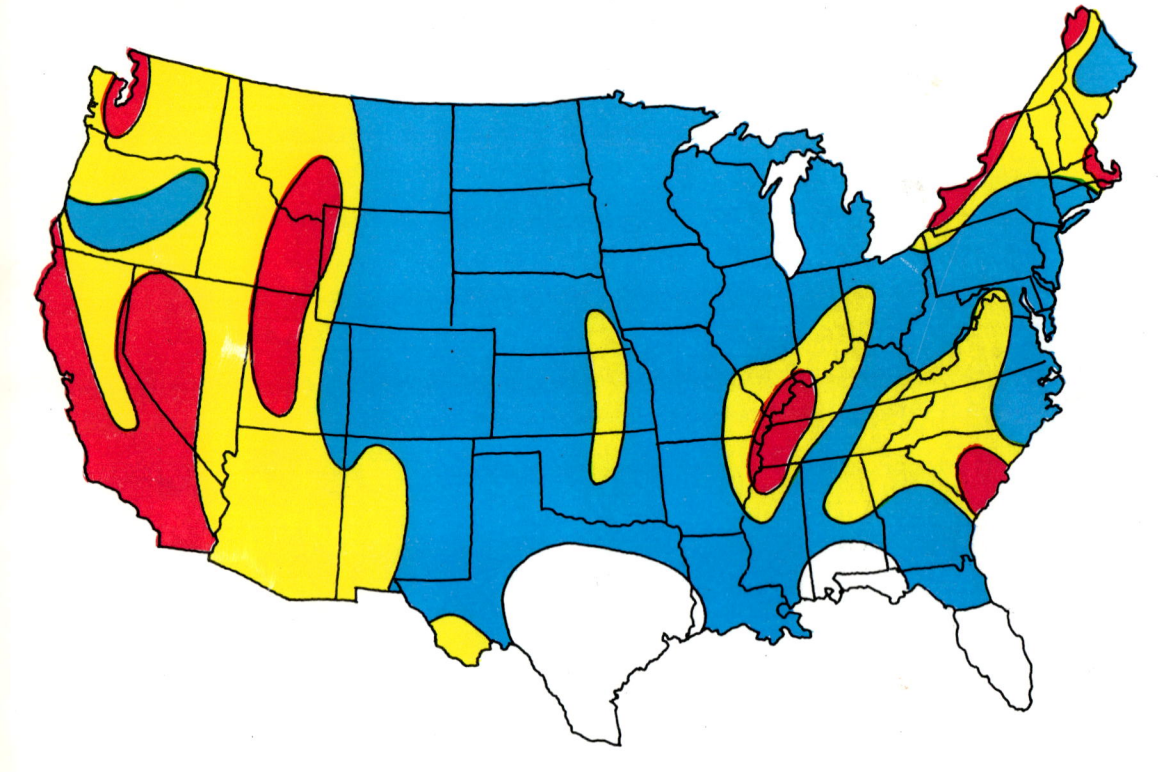

A *seismic risk* map shows areas and amounts of possible damage from earthquakes in the continental United States. Such information is based on history of earthquake activity as well as location of faults.

MAJOR EARTHQUAKE AREAS

Geological conditions within the earth's crust cause certain areas to have more earthquakes than others.

Geologically new and active areas of the earth, where there are tectonic conditions such as **plate subduction** and **lateral fault action**, tend to have earthquakes. For example, the west coasts of North and South America, the east coasts of Japan, and the South Pacific area have numerous quakes.

The Southern European countries of Turkey, Greece, Yugoslavia, and Italy, as well as areas around the Indian Ocean, are also likely spots for earthquakes to occur.

Now, humankind has added another type of seismic event: massive underground explosions that show up on a seismograph. The seismic motions from an underground explosion can be distinguished from those of an earthquake since the underground explosion produces a different wave pattern on the seismogram.

While areas of great seismic activity have more earthquakes, there are many other places on earth where occasional quakes do occur. Some seismologists even say there may not be *any* place on earth that can be considered free of seismic activity and earthquakes. See page 31.

geological	related to conditions and forces within the earth
geologically new	recently formed or changed within the last several million years
plate subduction	condition of one plate sliding under another
lateral fault action	movement of the face of one fault against another in a side-to-side motion

If exact earthquake prediction had been possible, people would have avoided this San Fernando underpass on the morning of February 9, 1971. Seismologists study the periods between seismic events, hoping to find patterns to help determine when a quake might happen.

WHEN WILL THE BIG ONE COME?

By studying the history of earthquakes in a given area, one can make some general or rough predictions. In an area of Southern California, for example, a severe (possibly Richter 8.0) earthquake has occurred once every 100-150 years. The last tremendous earthquake in Southern California was at Fort Tejon in 1857. So it's reasonable to say there is a good chance of an 8.0 quake in that portion of the San Andreas fault some time between now and the year 2007. And the closer we get to the end of that period, the more likely it is for the quake to occur.

There *are* some cases where we can make some quite definite predictions. If a quake has just occurred, it's very likely that aftershocks will follow. And if a very large earthquake has occurred recently, it will take a long time for the seismic pressure to build up for the next very big one.

Some think certain earthquakes can be predicted by **foreshocks**. But more often than not, a major quake has no foreshocks, and one can't always be sure if any seismic movement is an event by itself or a predictor of a larger event.

foreshock   smaller quake occurring ahead of the main quake

SURVIVAL GUIDE

BEFORE

It's a good idea to be prepared for any disaster, whether or not you live in an earthquake zone. Some say each family must be able to get along on its own for at least 3 days (72 hours). This means putting in a supply of 3 gallons of water per person, canned foods including fruits, vegetables, and meat, canned or dried milk, cereals, rice, and beans. A hand-operated can opener and some hand tools such as screw drivers and pliers are essential. A camping stove can be used for cooking, *but only outdoors*. Some people keep a special wrench hanging near the gas turnoff valve, in case of leaks. The wrench should have a handle long enough to give good leverage.

You can assemble a good first-aid kit in a tool box. Consult a survival guide for a list of medical supplies. A battery-operated radio is important for hearing public announcements and instructions.

Keep a sturdy pair of shoes and flashlight beside your bed because earthquakes can occur at night. Even if you are unhurt during the quake, you could cut your feet on broken glass after the shaking stops. It's also smart to have a set of evacuation clothes hanging in your closet: warm jacket, trousers, and shirt.

DURING

It's hard to think straight if you are wakened by the quake, but try to remain calm by snapping your fingers, praying, or shouting as you tell the earth to stop shaking. Here are some practical things to do *during* a quake. If inside, stay there and get away from windows. Cover your head and back of neck with a pillow, magazine, or book. It helps to get under a table or inside a strong doorway. If outside, stay there. Get away from high buildings, walls, power poles, and such. Inside a car is a good place, but avoid touching metal if any wires fall on the car. At a very high magnitude you may be unable to do any of these things or to change your location.

AFTER

After the quake wait for additional shocks. Do not light matches or switch on any lights, because you could cause a fire or an explosion of leaking gas. Keep your head and face protected as you check on other members of the family. Give any first-aid and check for fires and fire hazards, spilled chemicals, or fumes. Once your family is cared for, see if your neighbor needs help. Turn on your radio and listen for instructions. To keep from tying up telephone lines, use the phone only for emergencies.

EARTHQUAKES AND YOU

You can't keep an earthquake from happening, but you can be prepared for one or any other disaster. If you live in earthquake country, you can find a list of supplies needed after a major disaster by looking in your telephone directory, usually in the front or center of the book. Also study page 40 of this book.

Beyond all of this, you may decide right now to be a scientist who works in the field of earthquake technology. Will you be the one who designs a computer program to predict the aftermath of quakes of different magnitudes? Maybe you'll find a way to predict seismic events or design buildings to withstand an 8.0-magnitude quake. Someone in your family might become a volunteer: a block warden to give leadership in a disaster, a person trained in first-aid and other helping skills, or a ham operator. A young person of 10 or 11 can even be a runner who carries messages around the neighborhood.

In any case, the more you know, the better off you will be during the challenge of any natural disaster.

GLOSSARY

acceleration   gaining of speed—Negative acceleration means loss of speed, commonly called *deceleration*.

accelerograph   instrument to measure the acceleration of an object—In this case, the object is a portion of the earth's surface. See *acceleration*.

aftermath   time following a disastrous event

aftershock   lesser temblor following a big quake

asthenosphere   See *lithosphere* and page 7.

body wave   wave sent out by an earthquake which travels *through the earth* as opposed to surface waves that travel on the earth's surface

bracketed duration   length of time that earthquake level of shaking is above .05g—See *g*.

Celebes Islands   group of islands near the country of Malaysia

cholera   illness similar to typhoid fever, caused by water which is contaminated with human or animal wastes—See *typhoid fever* and *contamination*.

contamination   in this case, fouling of water so that it's no longer fit to drink

core   in this case, the central part of the earth below a depth of 2,900 kilometers—The core is thought to be molten iron with possibly a solid center.

creep   slow earth movement that doesn't produce an earthquake

deceleration   See *acceleration*.

detonated   set off to explode like a bomb

diameter   length of a line drawn from edge to edge through the center of a circle or sphere

duration   in this case, how long an earthquake lasts

epicenter	point on the earth's surface just above quake's focus—See *focus* and page 31.
faults	series of fractures, parts of which have moved in relation to each other
focus	starting point of the tear or rupture in earth's surface at the beginning of a quake
foreshock	smaller quake occurring ahead of the main quake
friction	sticking together of two surfaces because of their roughness
g	acceleration of a falling body—The pull of gravity causes a falling body to increase its speed by 35 kilometers per hour (22 miles per hour) every second, an acceleration of 1 g. For example, a falling body will be going 105 kilometers per hour (66 miles per hour) after three seconds.
geological	related to conditions and forces within the earth
geological time	span of the history of the earth as known today—about 4½ billion years
geologically new	recently formed or changed within the last several million years
ham radio operator	person with permit to operate a radio capable of sending messages a long distance
interplate earthquake	one occurring at plate boundaries—Plate motion can be dipping or side-to-side. See *subduction zone*.
lateral fault action	movement of the face of one fault against another in a side-to-side motion
lithosphere	hard, outer shell of the earth, consisting of a rocklike layer that is about 30 kilometers (50 miles) thick, resting on a fudgelike layer, the *asthenosphere*
magma	molten rock beneath earth's surface that becomes lava when it erupts and rock when it cools
magnitude	numerical measure of strength
mantle	main bulk of the earth between crust and core

P wave, primary	first and fastest body wave after the quake—P waves contract and release material in line with their forward movement through the earth. See *S wave*.
plate	large, rigid portion of the earth's lithosphere—See *lithosphere*.
plate subduction	condition of one plate sliding under another
plate tectonics	theory that earth's surface is made of plates that move, grow, and rub against each other—See *theory*.
power supplies	electricity-generating machines, usually powered by gas or diesel fuel
province	area similar to a state such as those in the United States
quantify	measure in a logical way, usually with numbers
Richter Scale	series of numbers used to describe earthquake strength. See *magnitude* and page 29.
rig	in this case, a ham radio
ruptured	torn open
S wave, secondary	body wave that follows P wave—S waves actually shove rocks and other material to the right and left of their direction of motion. See *P wave*.
San Andreas	fault along the west coast of Mexico and the U.S., located where the North American and Pacific Plates meet—It runs from northern Baja, Mexico, up through a large portion of California. See *fault* and *plate*.
seismic event	occurrence related to an earthquake
seismic wave	wave of energy traveling through the earth's interior or on its surface

seismogram	written record of a seismic event—See *seismic event*.
seismograph	instrument that records the earth's motions during a seismic event in the form of a written record—See *seismic event*.
seismologist	person who studies seismic action
73	ham radio way of saying "goodbye"
sign off	in this case, shut down the radio
spreading zone	area where plates are being driven apart and new plate material is formed from magma. See *magma*.
statistics	numbers for things such as damage and injuries related to a seismic event
subduction zone	area where a plate dips under another one, usually an area where deep earthquakes occur
temblor	shaking of the earth
theory	group of ideas to explain a phenomenon
tidal wave	unusually high wave caused by the action of ocean tides and wind—Tidal waves sometimes arrive onshore as the result of huge storms.
traces	lines of a seismogram that show waves from a seismic event—See *seismogram* and *seismic event*.
transmitting towers	tall structures from which radio and television messages are sent
tremor	small movement within the earth's crust
tsunami	Japanese word for "harbor wave," word for large wave generated by underwater seismic activity
typhoid fever	illness causing diarrhea, headache, fever, and possible death
unsung	not recognized nor heard of
wave	See *Body wave, P wave*, and *S wave*.
wroth	very angry

INDEX

acceleration, 33
accelerograph, 33
active, 13, 37
aftermath, 17, 41
aftershock, 14, 15, 39
Alaska, 15, 23, 26
Aleppo, Italy, 23
Aleutian Is., 15
Anchorage, Alaska, 23
asthenosphere, 7
Atlas, 9

batteries, 21, 40
Bible, 9
blood transfusions, 19
body wave, 31
bracketed duration, 33

California, 9, 12, 20-22, 26, 35, 39
California Indians, 9
catfish, 9
Celebes Islands, 9
China, 23, 27, 35
cholera, 17
clock, 32
Cocos Plate, 10, 11
communication, 17, 21
contamination, 17
core, 6, 7
creep, 13
Crescent City, CA, 35
crust, 7, 13, 37

damage, 19, 21, 22, 26, 27, 29, 33, 35, 36
danger, 19, 29
data, 31
deceleration, 33
detonated, 17
diameter, 7
doctors, 21
duration, 33

electric lines, 16, 17, 21, 40
engineers, 21
epicenter, 30, 31, 33
evacuation, 40
explosion, 17, 37, 40

fault, 12, 13, 15, 23, 36, 39
fire, 17, 23, 40
fire fighters, 19
first-aid, 17, 40, 41
focus, 31
foreshocks, 39
Fort Tejon, CA, 39
friction, 13

g, 33
geological, 37
geological time, 13, 36
geologically new, 37
Greece, 37
Greeks, 9

ham radio operator, 20, 21, 41
Hawaii, 35
hazards, 17, 40
heroes, 18, 19, 21
historic earthquakes, 23
Hong Kong, 35
Honshu, Japan, 34

inactive, 13
Indian Ocean, 37
Indian Plate, 7
intensity, 27
interplate earthquake, 11
Italy, 23, 37

Japan, Japanese, 8, 34, 37

Kansu, 23

lateral fault action, 37
layers, 7
legends, 9
lithosphere, 7, 11, 13
location, 31, 36, 40

magma, 11
magnitude, 5, 25, 27-31, 40, 41
Malaysia, 9
mantle, 7
maps, 10, 12, 36
measurement, 27, 29, 33
medical people, supplies, 19, 21, 40
Mercalli Scale, 27
Mexico, 4, 5, 10, 11, 18-20, 23
motion detection, 24

namazu, 8
No. American Plate, 7, 10, 11, 23
No. & So. America, 23, 37
nurses, 21
nuclear blast, 30

oceans, 10, 11

P wave, primary, 30, 31
Pacific Ocean, 10
Pacific Plate, 7, 11, 23
planet, 6, 7
plate, 7, 10-13
plate subduction, 37
plate tectonics, 7
police, 19
power supplies, 21
prediction, 5, 35, 38, 39, 41
province, 23

quantify, 27

radio, 20, 21, 40
rescue workers, 19
Richter, Charles, 28
Richter Scale, 5, 23, 28, 29, 39
rig, 21
rubble, 19
ruptured, 17

S wave, secondary, 30, 31
Saint Francis Hotel, 12, 22
San Andreas, 23, 39
San Fernando, CA, 14, 26, 32, 38

San Francisco, CA, 12, 13, 22, 23, 29
scientist, 7, 9, 41
seismic event, 15, 25, 27, 35, 37, 38, 41
seismic risk map, 36
seismic risk, 36
seismic waves, 23
seismogram, 25, 30, 31, 37
seismograph, 15, 24, 25, 31, 33, 37
seismologist, 27, 29-31, 33, 36-38
seventy-three (73), 21
sewer lines, 17
Shensi, China, 23
sign off, 21
Soltys, Robert G., 20
So. California, 39
So. Europe, 37
So. Pacific, 37
spreading zone, 11
statistics, 27
subduction zone, 11
survival guide, 40

"tablequake," 25
Tangshan, China, 23
tectonics, 7, 13
telephone, 21, 40, 41
television, 21
temblor, 15, 17
theory, 7, 9, 15
tidal wave, 5, 34, 35
trace, 25, 30
transfusion, 19
transmitting towers, 21
tremor, 11
tsunami, 34, 35
Turkey, 37
typhoid fever, 17

underground explosion, 37
unsung, 19

volunteer, 41

warning centers, 35
water, 17, 19, 40
Wegener, Alfred, 7
wroth, 9

Yugoslavia, 37

47

THE AUTHORS

Ed Radlauer, graduate of the University of California at Los Angeles and Whittier College, former teacher, reading specialist, and school administrator, has authored, co-authored, edited, and illustrated over 200 books for young people. Subject areas range from Aircraft to Zion National Park. He has always been interested in technology and science, so writing about earthquakes has been of great interest. While his homes are near the San Andreas and San Jacinto faults in California, he calmly goes about his hobbies which include radio, electronics and cooking. His wife, Ruth, says he's a terrific low-sugar, low-salt, low-fat cook.

Ruth Radlauer, Editor of Elk Grove Books, is the originator of the Geo Books and has authored and co-authored nine titles in the series. She is the author of 20 books about the national parks as well as co-author with her husband of more than 150 other books ranging in subjects from volcanoes to gymnastics and rock climbing to robots. Ruth and her son Dan collaborate on the creation of musicals for young people to perform. The Radlauers live in La Habra Heights, and Idyllwild, California.